# FOREWORD

*by W. P. Mara, author of the companion volume* **Milk Snakes, Every Species and Subspecies in Brilliant Color**

The snakes of the genus *Lampropeltis* have done more to intrigue and fascinate herpetocultural hobbyists than any other serpent group in the world (although the boas and pythons, plus the ever-popular Corn Snakes, undoubtedly are right behind). Known in English as the kingsnakes and Milk Snakes, these animals possess all the traits enthusiasts hold most dear—they are remarkably attractive, many being endowed with rich reds, radiant yellows, and bold blacks while others boast handsome browns and ashy, earthy grays; they are small and thus very manageable; they are easy to tame (most don't need to be tamed in the first place); and they are undemanding in their requirements for housing, feeding, and, most importantly in this day and age, breeding. There are albinos and melanistics and color phases and pattern varieties, etc., etc., etc. In short, they've got it all.

So why not a book or two? And why not a *good* book or two? Since I wrote the "other" one, I can't pass judgment on it, but I didn't write this one, so I can.

Ron Markel knows his stuff. He's a keeper of kingsnakes, a breeder of kingsnakes, and, best of all, a *fan* of kingsnakes. He knows about their taxonomy, their natural history, how they breed, what they eat, where they live. He's collected them, photographed them, written pages of notes about them, and therefore is, in every sense of the word, an expert.

The book you're holding has enough information to guide you through every step of kingsnake husbandry and propagation. It is thoughtfully written and nicely illustrated. It is, indeed, a worthy product that will serve its purpose without shame. Truly, you are getting your money's worth, and these days, that's really something.

Enjoy it.

"BLOTCHED KINGSNAKE," *Lampropeltis getula "goini."* The kingsnakes and the Milk Snakes, genus *Lampropeltis*, undoubtedly make the finest captives. Attractive and easy to breed, they are the very apex of collectable herptiles.

PHOTO BY R. D. BARTLETT.

PHOTO BY K. T. NEMURAS.

"BLAIR'S KINGSNAKE," *Lampropeltis alterna "blairi."* One of the more attractive, and more popular, of the kingsnakes, Blair's King simply is a color form of the equally popular Gray-banded Kingsnake, *Lampropeltis alterna.*

# NATURAL HISTORY & TAXONOMY

Some snakes have very little information published as to details such as precise subspecies or ranges. However, the kingsnakes, of the genus *Lampropeltis*, have been heavily studied and the ensuing data have been published for numerous years. Since the very earliest descriptions, *Lampropeltis* species and subspecies have undergone constant reclassification which in turn has kept them up to date.

## TAXONOMY AND ETYMOLOGY

Rather than go into lengthy discussions of original descriptions, I have opted to go with what is most current, categorizing each subspecies with only the most recent and revised Latin nomenclature.

The three most recent spelling changes in this book, also mentioned in my first book, *Kingsnakes and Milk Snakes* (TFH 1990, TS-125), are *Lampropeltis getulus* now being *Lampropeltis getula*; *Lampropeltis g. niger* going to *Lampropeltis g. nigra*; and *Lampropeltis g. nigritus* going to *Lampropeltis g. nigrita*.

*Lampropeltis* is derived from the Greek *lampros* meaning shiny, and *pelta* which means shield or scales, thus, **shiny scales**. The group belongs to the family Colubridae and is characterized by smooth scales and paired apical pits. Species recognized in this book as currently valid are ***L. alterna*** (no subspecies but with one problematical form); ***L. calligaster*** (three subspecies); ***L.***

CALIFORNIA KINGSNAKE, *Lampropeltis getula californiae*. Most of the kingsnakes are native to the United States, but a few can also be found in Mexican regions. This subspecies is native to both—over most of California, Oregon, Nevada, Utah, and Arizona, then south into northern Mexico including Baja.

*getula* (seven subspecies with six problematical forms), ***L. mexicana*** (no subspecies but with two problematical forms which are still being looked at by a number of individuals as possible valid subspecies), and ***L. ruthveni*** (no subspecies).

## BASIC GEOGRAPHY

Kingsnakes occur exclusively in the United States and Mexico. The Gray-banded Kingsnake, *L. alterna*, is found in southwestern Texas and then south into Coahuila and Durango. The Prairie Kingsnake, *L. calligaster*, ranges over most of the southeastern quarter of the U. S. and then west into the prairie regions beyond the Mississippi River. The Common Kingsnake, *L. getula*, primarily is found in the southern half of the U. S., from coast to coast (plus Baja and Mexico). The San Luis Potosi Kingsnake, *L. mexicana*, occurs mainly in the Saladan region of the Chihuahuan Desert with a few further reported localities nearby. Finally, Ruthven's Kingsnake, *L. ruthveni*, which is now being called the Queretaro Kingsnake by many, is the most southerly ranging kingsnake, found on the Mexican Plateau on Michoacan, Queretaro, and Jalisco.

## HABITAT

Kingsnakes, being so well distributed, occur in a variety of habitats, including swamps, fields, forest, mountains, desert, and valleys; basically anywhere weather conditions permit.

"BLOTCHED KINGSNAKE," *Lampropeltis getula "goini."* Due to the immense variation of many of the kingsnakes, identification of specimens sometimes is quite difficult. They even vary between adults and young. This juvenile, for example, probably will lose most of its orange tinting by its third year.

PHOTO BY R. G. MARKEL.

PHOTO BY W. P. MARA.

Above: SAN LUIS POTOSI KINGSNAKE, *Lampropeltis mexicana*. This is an unusual "golden phase" variant of the San Luis Potosi King. In normally colored specimens, the ground color is more grayish, like that of the anterior portion of the head. Below: EASTERN KINGSNAKE, *Lampropeltis getula getula*. Specimen caught in funnel trap in the New Jersey Pine Barrens. Note the sandy, loamy soil that beds this habitat.

PHOTO BY R. T. ZAPPALORTI.

## GENERAL IDENTIFICATION

Kingsnakes can be identified by a number of distinct features, basically morphological. Size is one means of identification. With an average body length of 3 ft/ 91 cm to 6 ft/183 cm, they are classified as small to moderate in size. They also have relatively short tails. The dorsal scales are arranged in 17 to 27 rows. The anal plate is single while the subcaudals are divided. The hemipenis is asymmetrically bilobed, either distinctly or shallowly. Patterns vary and are described in each subspecies account.

**"DURANGO MOUNTAIN KINGSNAKE,"** *Lampropeltis mexicana "greeri."* The taxonomy of most of the kingsnakes is fairly solid, but some, like this color form of the San Luis Potosi Kingsnake, *L. mexicana*, have been confusing both scientists and hobbyists for decades. Is it a valid subspecies or not? That, truly, is the question.

# SPECIES, SUBSPECIES, AND THE "ODDBALLS"

I have endeavored to make the following list of kingsnake species and subspecies as complete as possible, taking into account all of the most relevant and up-to-date literature. I have also attempted to design my taxonomic views in a reasonable, rational fashion, with the hopes of reflecting those most often subscribed to in today's herpetological community.

The arrangement is simple—first the animal's name in English and then Latin, and then the author of the Latin and the date of authorship. After that, a general description of the animal, followed by some natural history and miscellanea, and finally, the geographic range. Coverage of the animals runs alphabetically according to the name of the species first, and then the subspecies.

Toward the end of the chapter the most common problematical kingsnake forms (the "oddballs" that give taxonomists migraines) are discussed, covering both their origin and their identification, the latter of which is sometimes inherently difficult since many animals are problematical due to the fact that they are tough to diagnose in the first place.

## GRAY-BANDED KINGSNAKE
### *Lampropeltis alterna*
(Brown, 1901)

To herpetoculturists, this is one of the most sought-after snakes in the world. A moderate-sized

GRAY-BANDED KINGSNAKE, *Lampropeltis alterna.* Notice the complete reduction of reddish orange coloring on the saddles of this specimen. Many believe this to be a result of the animal's mimicry of a sympatric rattlesnake (the Banded Rock Rattlesnake, *Crotalus lepidus klauberi*).

PHOTO BY R. G. MARKEL.

**GRAY-BANDED KINGSNAKE,** *Lampropeltis alterna.* Although immensely popular in the herpetocultural hobby, newborns of the Gray-banded King have a high mortality rate. Because of this, many professional culturists have removed the species from their breeding programs.

PHOTO BY K. H. SWITAK.

serpent, adults reach about 4 ft/ 122 cm. It is best described as having an ashy gray ground color, with reddish orange saddles outlined first with black and then white. These saddles are sometimes quite thin, often to the point where the orange coloring is totally obscured, and they number somewhere between 15 and 39. The snake's eye is relatively large and the iris is silvery gray (one characteristic that separates it from *L. mexicana*). It also has a fairly high ventral count—210 to 232.

Undescribed until 1901, the Gray-banded Kingsnake is a nocturnal creature that does remarkably well in captivity as an adult, feeding on mice and small rats and reproducing without trouble, but newborns are often difficult to get feeding (small lizards only) and their mortality rate is heart-breakingly high.

Range: Southwestern Texas

PHOTO BY R. G. MARKEL.

GRAY-BANDED KINGSNAKE, *Lampropeltis alterna*. Found only from southwestern Texas to northern Mexico, Gray-banded Kings are becoming rarer and rarer due to the droves of collectors who travel to their locality each year and literally grab dozens of them.

and northern Mexico (Coahuila, Durango).

GRAY-BANDED KINGSNAKE, *Lampropeltis alterna*. A somewhat unusual specimen in that it has broad saddles but with no reddish orange coloration.

PHOTO BY R. G. MARKEL.

PHOTO BY GEROLD P. MERKER.

GRAY-BANDED KINGSNAKE, *Lampropeltis alterna*. Most Gray-bands are remarkably attractive, but some, like the specimen shown, have a broken, irregular pattern and very little in the way of bright coloring. Such specimens often can be purchased at relatively lower prices and still produce nicely colored specimens later on.

## PRAIRIE KINGSNAKE
### *Lampropeltis calligaster calligaster*
(Harlan, 1827)

Can attain a length of about 50 in/127 cm. There are around 60 reddish or greenish blotches, squarish in shape and with black edges, usually with concave margins. Sometimes the blotches may be split into two separate rows. Ground color will be a brown, light tan, or even a pinkish color. Belly is yellow with dark, square blotches. Young often are strongly spotted.

Occurs in open fields and prairies and lightly wooded areas. Average of 11 eggs per clutch. This subspecies appears relatively calm and does well in captivity. Striped specimens have been collected and reproduced in captivity, as have albino and striped albino forms.

Range: Indiana west to Nebraska, south through the Mississippi Valley to eastern Texas and western Louisiana.

PRAIRIE KINGSNAKE, *Lampropeltis calligaster calligaster*. Artwork by John R. Quinn.

PRAIRIE KINGSNAKE, *Lampropeltis calligaster calligaster*. The Prairie Kingsnake is not as popular as some of the other kings, but certainly makes a superb captive. Most specimens thrive on a diet of mice and display the mildest of tempers. Shown is an uncommon striped specimen.

PHOTO BY R. G. MARKEL

PHOTO BY R. G. MARKEL.

Above: PRAIRIE KINGSNAKE, *Lampropeltis calligaster calligaster*. Notice the clearly defined V-shape on the top of the Prairie King's head. Notice also the very dark dorsal markings on the considerably lighter background. Both traits are characteristic of this animal. Below: An easy captive to both house and feed, the Prairie King is strikingly beautiful in its juvenile form, as shown here.

PHOTO BY R. G. MARKEL.

PRAIRIE KINGSNAKE, *Lampropeltis calligaster calligaster*. Like so many of the popular kingsnakes, the Prairie King is bred in an albino form. The specimen shown is of this type and is also laterally striped, a trait uncommon to this animal.

PHOTO BY R. G. MARKEL.

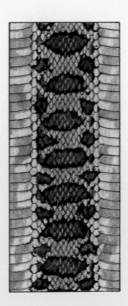

SOUTH FLORIDA MOLE SNAKE, *Lampropeltis calligaster occipitolineata*. Artwork by John R. Quinn.

## SOUTH FLORIDA MOLE SNAKE
***Lampropeltis calligaster occipitolineata***
Price, 1987

This is the most recently described kingsnake. It has many of the characters of the Prairie Kingsnake, but is differentiated by a high number of body blotches (78 to 79) combined with a dorsal scale row count of 21. There also is a network of dark lines down the back of the head. Many still consider this subspecies problematical, but it probably is valid.

Range: Specimens are known only from Okeechobee and Brevard County, Florida. These localities are far south from the most southerly known locale of *L. c. rhombomaculata*. Other localities are now suspected as well.

PHOTO BY R. D. BARTLETT.

SOUTH FLORIDA MOLE SNAKE, *Lampropeltis calligaster occipitolineata*. The "newest" of the kingsnakes (described only in 1987), this taxon is considered by some to be problematical, but most experts have accepted it as valid. Specimens in the herpetocultural trade are uncommon and usually command a high price.

## MOLE SNAKE
***Lampropeltis calligaster rhombomaculata***
(Holbrook, 1840)

Average adult length is somewhere around 48 in/122 cm. Ground color usually a medium to dark brown, with dorsal blotching of a dark mahogany red color. These blotches tend to have convex or straight anterior and posterior margins. Half-grown and large specimens sometimes have a complete loss of pattern.

This is a snake of woodlots, cultivated areas, and other open fields. It is an inveterate burrower and comes out only during the night or immediately after rainstorms. Prefers both mammals and reptiles as food.

Range: Maryland to northern Florida, west to Tennessee and southeastern Louisiana.

MOLE SNAKE, *Lampropeltis calligaster rhombomaculata*. Artwork by John R. Quinn.

PHOTO BY R. G. MARKEL.

Above: MOLE SNAKE, *Lampropeltis calligaster rhombomaculata*. Although undeniably a beautiful animal, the Mole Snake is quite secretive, most specimens being found only during the night hours or after warm rains. Below: MOLE SNAKE, *Lampropeltis calligaster rhombomaculata*. In older specimens of the Mole Snake, the attractive saddle pattern fades and sometimes vanishes completely.

PHOTO BY R. D. BARTLETT.

## CALIFORNIA KINGSNAKE
*Lampropeltis getula californiae*
(Blainville, 1835)

Adults can attain a length of about 60 in/152 cm. Ground color can be either a chocolate brown or a simple black. Pattern varies from being longitudinally striped to barred or ringed. Color of stripes or bars can be either plain white or banana yellow. There are many other varieties as well (including the breeder-cultured "banana king," which, in quality specimens, is all yellow), but the handful of combinations of the traits already mentioned are the basic forms. The most sought-after phase in the herpetocultural hobby is the black-with-white-rings variety. Dorsal scale rows 23 to 25, ventrals 213 to 255, subcaudals 44 to 63, supralabials 7 to 8, infralabials 9 to 10, and rings or bars, when present, 21 to 44.

Albinos have been bred for dozens of years in banded, striped, and aberrant varieties. Common in

CALIFORNIA KINGSNAKE, *Lampropeltis getula californiae*. The banded variant of the California Kingsnake, shown here, is known to some as "Boyle's Banded Kingsnake," (*Lampropeltis getula "boyli"*).

captivity due its gentle nature, ease of breeding, and ability to adapt to captivity (it has aggressive and very reliable feeding habits). Due to the great number of pattern and color variations, which can be credited largely to distribution, there are a number of problematical forms of this animal (which are discussed later).

Range: Oregon to southern Utah, Nevada, Arizona, California, and the Baja Peninsula, Mexico.

MOLE SNAKE, *Lampropeltis calligaster rhombomaculata*. The Mole Snake earned its common name from its burrowing, mole-like habits, plus the fact that many will feed on moles, hence a further, and now-defunct, common name, the "Mole Catcher."

 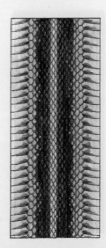  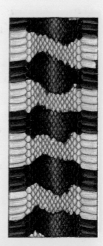

CALIFORNIA KINGSNAKE, *Lampropeltis getula californiae*. Striped variety. Artwork by John R. Quinn.

CALIFORNIA KINGSNAKE, *Lampropeltis getula californiae*. Banded variety. Artwork by John R. Quinn.

CALIFORNIA KINGSNAKE, *Lampropeltis getula californiae*. Due to the Cal King's immense popularity, albino forms are common in the herpetocultural trade. They are in fact so common that newborns can be obtained at relatively low prices.

PHOTO BY K. T. NEMURAS.

PHOTO BY R. G. MARKEL.

CALIFORNIA KINGSNAKE, *Lampropeltis getula californiae.* Specimens of both the banded and the striped versions of the California Kingsnake can be found sympatrically in southern California and northern Baja. The animal shown below, incidentally, is remarkable in that its vertebral stripe is perfect (i.e., unbroken).

PHOTO BY W. P. MARA.

CALIFORNIA KINGSNAKE, *Lampropeltis getula californiae*. Geographically speaking, the ringed variant of the Cal King is the more common of the two due to the fact that it occurs over the majority of the range. Striped specimens, however, seem more popular with hobbyists.

Above: CALIFORNIA KINGSNAKE, *Lampropeltis getula californiae*. Highly melanistic specimen. Below: CALIFORNIA KINGSNAKE, *Lampropeltis getula californiae*. A litter of neonates that were produced from one striped parent and one banded parent. Although Cal Kings of this kind are sold in the hobby they are not terribly popular, probably due to their irregular patterns.

CALIFORNIA KINGSNAKE, *Lampropeltis getula californiae*. Aberrations in both color and pattern are fairly common in captive-bred Cal Kings. Above, an adult specimen appears to be strongly melanistic with a highly fractured pattern. Below, the animal shows no melanistic tendencies and the pattern is only slightly aberrant.

## FLORIDA KINGSNAKE
*Lampropeltis getula floridana*
Blanchard, 1919

This subspecies reaches a length of around 60 in/152 cm, and the most common form can be diagnosed by the presence of 22 to 66 light, orange to yellow crosslines on a dark brown to almost black ground color. The belly is cream or pale yellow with tan or pinkish brown spots. The young have stronger light colors than the adults and sometimes have a little red or orange tinting, but otherwise resemble their parents exactly.

This animal has been recorded as a native of cypress ponds and savannah pinelands, and also is known to inhabit other sandy, open areas. It keeps itself fairly inconspicuous for a kingsnake and is popular with hobbyists, having been bred many times in captivity. There is an albino form available, albeit only rarely, but it is not as visually compelling as many of the other albino kingsnakes.

Range: Southern and southwestern Florida, with isolated populations in northeastern Florida and the Panhandle. In the northern and central parts of the state it intergrades heavily with *L. g. getula.*

FLORIDA KINGSNAKE, *Lampropeltis getula floridana*. A popular pet with hobbyists, newborn specimens show a particular fondness for small mice, which makes them easier to raise than their northern relative the Eastern King, *L. g. getula*, which often has a marked preference for tiny snakes and lizards.

PHOTO BY K. T. NEMURAS.

PHOTO BY R. G. MARKEL.

Above: FLORIDA KINGSNAKE, *Lampropeltis getula floridana*. Specimen showing the "standard" Florida King color and pattern—yellowish "chains" with a darker background. Below: A "BLOTCHED KINGSNAKE," *Lampropeltis getula "goini."* This variety of the Florida King is diagnosed by its high amount of yellowish gold and, unlike the other Florida King variety, *L. g. "brooksi,"* it has a visibly blotched pattern.

PHOTO BY R. D. BARTLETT.

**FLORIDA KINGSNAKE,** *Lampropeltis getula floridana.* Only described in 1919, the Florida King is a fairly secretive creature but seems locally abundant. Until restrictions were applied to collectors, it was not unusual for a talented field worker to obtain two dozen specimens in a single weekend.

## EASTERN KINGSNAKE
### *Lampropeltis getula getula*
(Linnaeus, 1766)

Also known as the Chain Kingsnake, this is one of the largest and most heavy-bodied of the *getula* group. It has a distinct "chain-like" pattern ("net-like" has also been used in descriptions) colored in white or cream. There usually are 15 to 44 of these markings on a dark brown or black ground color. Record adult length is 82 in/208.3 cm. Average is somewhere around 48 in/122 cm.

The Eastern King normally occurs in an aquatic or swamp-type environment. It is a voracious eater of mammals, but many keepers have complained that their specimens would only take other reptiles rather than the easier-to-acquire, furry, warm-blooded prey. The young in particular seem addicted to dietary items that are difficult for the average herpetoculturist to supply. Nevertheless, hardy specimens are long-lived and tame down nicely, becoming safe hand decorations and intriguing terrarium subjects. They also are easy to breed and have been produced through dozens of generations in captivity.

Range: Southern New Jersey to West Virginia, south to northern Florida, and west to the Appalachians and southeastern Alabama.

EASTERN KINGSNAKE, *Lampropeltis getula getula*. A beautiful animal that occurs in a wide variety of habitats, the Eastern King is a favorite among hobbyists. It is a calm, gentle creature that breeds easily in captivity, and most adults can be relied upon to feed on rodents. Newborns, however, may be a little more inclined to want tiny reptiles.

PHOTO BY R. G. MARKEL.

PHOTO BY JOHN IVERSON.

**EASTERN KINGSNAKE,** *Lampropeltis getula getula.* Found only in the eastern United States from southern New Jersey south to northern Florida (including the Panhandle), many Eastern Kings spend their winters hibernating not in mammal burrows like other colubrids, but in swamps.

 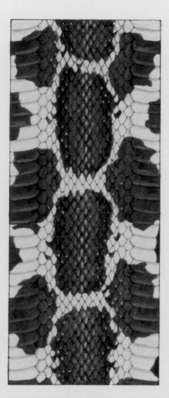

EASTERN KINGSNAKE, *Lampropeltis getula getula*. Artwork by John R. Quinn.

EASTERN KINGSNAKE, *Lampropeltis getula getula*. It should be noted that due to the Eastern King's strongly ophiophagus (snake-eating) nature, it should be housed alone or, at the very most, with a specimen of equal size and of the *same species* (and, even then, only during the breeding season).

PHOTO BY MARK SMITH.

## SPECKLED KINGSNAKE
### *Lampropeltis getula holbrooki*
Stejneger, 1902

Sometimes called the "Salt and Pepper Kingsnake," this subspecies is easily recognized by a single light dot on each dark scale. On many of the ventrolateral scales the light coloration is so prominent it almost obscures the dark completely. In some specimens there is a light cross-lining, giving the animal a vague resemblance to *L. g. getula.* Average adult length is around 48 in/122 cm.

At the western side of this animal's range, in central Texas, it sometimes intergrades with *L. g. splendida.* In the east it does the same with *nigra.* Habitats vary from open prairies and grasslands to upland woodlands and even swamps. Albino forms have been produced in captivity although they have not enjoyed a high degree of popularity.

Range: Southwestern Illinois to southern Iowa, south to eastern Texas, then east to southwestern Alabama.

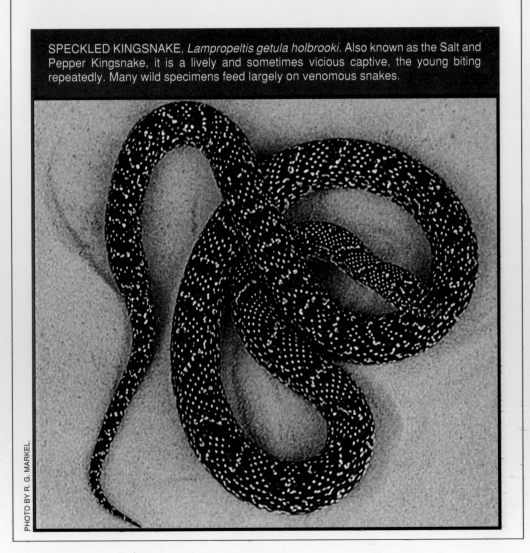

SPECKLED KINGSNAKE, *Lampropeltis getula holbrooki*. Also known as the Salt and Pepper Kingsnake, it is a lively and sometimes vicious captive, the young biting repeatedly. Many wild specimens feed largely on venomous snakes.

PHOTO BY R. G. MARKEL.

PHOTO BY GLEN CARLZEN.

SPECKLED KINGSNAKE, *Lampropeltis getula holbrooki*. Above: Albino variety, very cleanly patterned, which is unusual for albinos of this animal. Below: Another neatly marked specimen, this one lacking the vague chain-link arrangement found in many specimens.

PHOTO BY R. G. MARKEL.

## BLACK KINGSNAKE
### *Lampropeltis getula nigra*
(Yarrow, 1882)

Mostly black but not uniform, this kingsnake has the faintest hint of the light-colored dorsal cross-lining so obvious in snakes like *L. g. getula*. The belly is marked with both white and black with no distinct direction or form to the pattern. Average adult length is between 36 and 45 in/91 and 114 cm.

Found in wooded areas, stream edges, and places where mankind has left a heavy mark, this is not one of the more popular kingsnakes, probably due to its lack of beauty in comparison to the other kings. The Black Desert Kingsnake, *L. g. nigrita*, for example, also is uniformly black but in a much "cleaner" manner and thus it is more appealing to the eye.

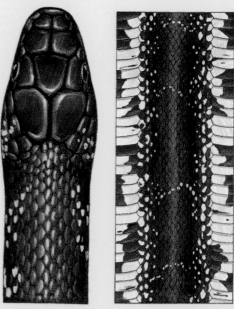

BLACK KINGSNAKE, *Lampropeltis getula nigra.* Artwork by John R. Quinn.

Range: Southern Ohio to southeastern Illinois, then south to central Alabama and northwestern Georgia.

BLACK KINGSNAKE, *Lampropeltis getula nigra.* Most kingsnakes can be relied upon to eat small mammals or, at the very least, other reptiles. However, in 1933 a Tennessee specimen of the Black Kingsnake was discovered eating turtle eggs from a pondside nest. Eggs of both reptiles and birds are known to be a part of some kingsnakes' diets.

PHOTO BY GLEN CARLZEN.

## BLACK DESERT KINGSNAKE
*Lampropeltis getula nigrita*
Zweifel and Norris, 1955

A popular kingsnake in private collections, this beautiful animal is a glossy jet black on both the top and bottom (although there are the occasional rare specimens that exhibit some vague, light-colored patterning on both the belly and dorsum). Juveniles may exhibit some faint pattern, but with each shed they turn darker and darker. Average adult length for the snake is between 24 and 36 in/61 and 91 cm.

The Black Desert King interbreeds with both *L. g. splendida* and *L. g. californiae* where their ranges overlap (in Arizona). It is primarily a nocturnal desert-dweller and does remarkably well in captivity, most specimens requiring little more than the most basic kingsnake care. With time, patience, and

BLACK DESERT KINGSNAKE, *Lampropeltis getula nigrita*. Artwork by John R. Quinn.

much handling, Black Desert Kings can also become tame to the point where they could be considered completely safe. They are, all around, superb examples of the kingsnake clan.

Range: Western Sonora and northwestern Sinaloa, Mexico.

BLACK DESERT KINGSNAKE, *Lampropeltis getula nigrita*. The Black Desert Kingsnake, also known to many as the Mexican Black Kingsnake, can be maintained with the most basic of captive care. Most hatchlings will feed on newborn mice.

PHOTO BY R. G. MARKEL.

PHOTO BY K. H. SWITAK.

BLACK DESERT KINGSNAKE, *Lampropeltis getula nigrita* × DESERT KINGSNAKE, *Lampropeltis getula splendida*. In a small region of Arizona there exists naturally occurring crossbreed populations of these two attractive snakes. Many resemble the shiny, vaguely patterned animal shown here.

## DESERT KINGSNAKE
*Lampropeltis getula splendida*
(Baird and Girard, 1853)

An overall dark black or brown ground color with white to yellow crossbars that may count as low as 42 or as high as 97. Most of the dark scales also consistently have yellow spotting. Average adult length usually is around 60 in/152 cm, making this one of the larger kingsnakes. Dorsal scale rows number between 23 and 25, ventrals 199 to 237, subcaudals 40 to 62, supralabials 7 to 8, infralabials 9 to 10.

DESERT KINGSNAKE, *Lampropeltis getula splendida*. Artwork by John R. Quinn.

Habitats for this creature include deserts, irrigated fields, and some areas where streams occur. It interbreeds with both *L. g. californiae* and *L. g. nigrita* in Arizona and extreme northern Mexico, and also with *L. g. holbrooki* to the east and north. Most specimens are carelessly and sloppily patterned, but choice specimens are exquisitely beautiful.

Range: Central Texas to southeastern Arizona, south to San Luis Potosi and Zacatecas, then west to Sonora and Santa Catalina Island in the Gulf of California.

DESERT KINGSNAKE, *Lampropeltis getula splendida*. A specimen somewhat high in the lighter colors, but with the typically dark *splendida* head. Specimens with brilliant colors like this are prized by collectors.

PHOTO BY K. H. SWITAK.

DESERT KINGSNAKE, *Lampropeltis getula splendida*. One of the more popular hobby kingsnakes, the Desert King has a broad range that overlaps many other subspecies, producing a number of intergrades. Captives do well, feeding on small mammals even for their first meal, but often have short tempers and may need repeated handlings before calming down.

BOTH PHOTOS BY R. G. MARKEL.

## SAN LUIS POTOSI KINGSNAKE
*Lampropeltis mexicana*
(Garman, 1884)

At an average adult length of 36 in/91 cm, this is one of the more moderate-sized kingsnakes. It is also one of the most beautiful, with a ground color of ashy light gray and saddles of orange-mahogany with dark edges. Sometimes there are alternating and reduced markings between the main blotches. What sets it apart from *L. alterna* is a large eye with a yellowish brown iris (it should be noted that at one time this snake and *L. alterna* were considered to be the same species). Also, the ventral count for *mexicana* is between 190 and 212, which is relatively lower than that of *alterna*.

A creature of oak/pine forests and meadows there are so many taxonomic problems with this animal that they're not even worth trying to tackle in a small book

SAN LUIS POTOSI KINGSNAKE, *Lampropeltis mexicana*. Artwork by John R. Quinn.

such as this. There seems to be an endless array of color and pattern variations, possible interbreeding, and other factors as well.

Range: Found mostly in the mountains edging the Chihuahuan Desert in northeastern Mexico.

SAN LUIS POTOSI KINGSNAKE, *Lampropeltis mexicana*. One of the most sought-after snakes among herpetoculturists, the San Luis Potosi King is also one of the most baffling, especially to taxonomists. There are countless color varieties, and exactly where each of these belongs in the big taxonomic picture is still a mystery.

PHOTO BY R. G. MARKEL.

PHOTO BY W. P. MARA.

Above: SAN LUIS POTOSI KINGSNAKE, *Lampropeltis mexicana*. Young example of a rare golden variety with greatly reduced saddles. Below: "DURANGO MOUNTAIN KINGSNAKE", *Lampropeltis mexicana "greeri."* Whether or not this snake is a valid subspecies is constantly in debate. Most consider it nothing more than a color variety, but one that is much prized by collectors.

PHOTO BY MELLA PANZELLA.

## RUTHVEN'S KINGSNAKE
*Lampropeltis ruthveni*
Blanchard, 1920

Difficult to define. This snake has a distinct Milk Snake pattern (*L. triangulum*) and in fact was at one time considered part of that group. The head is largely black but usually has some large red patches on it. If you look closely you will see that the black rings are bordered in lime green while the white rings are turn to tan ventrolaterally (two traits that are somewhat difficult to spot in casual photographs). The white, black, and red rings are fairly narrow, and the black rings do not dorsally encroach the red rings. Belly pattern is also red, white, and black. Adults reach 36 in/91 cm.

An unusual kingsnake species by having no subspecies, there are more than a few taxonomists who have no idea where this animal actually belongs. As

RUTHVEN'S KINGSNAKE, *Lampropeltis ruthveni* (also known as the QUERETARO KINGSNAKE). Artwork by John R. Quinn.

mentioned already, it was once thought to be a Milk Snake and only recently was given its own species. Albino forms have been produced in captivity, most of which are staggeringly beautiful and alarmingly expensive. This

RUTHVEN'S KINGSNAKE, *Lampropeltis ruthveni*. One of the lesser-studied kingsnakes, it was for many years classified as a Milk Snake, *Lampropeltis triangulum*. In truth, close investigation of the animal shows it to be most closely related to the San Luis Potosi King, *Lampropeltis mexicana*.

PHOTO BY D. BREIDENBACH.

PHOTO BY W. P. MARA.

**R U T H V E N ' S K I N G S N A K E , *Lampropeltis ruthveni*.** More and more specimens of this attractive snake are appearing in the herpetocultural hobby. An albino variety even exists, although examples currently are very expensive. Ruthven's King is fairly easy to maintain and propagate, and has a very mild temper.

animal is a native of wooded, rocky uplands.

Range: Mexican Plateau in Jalisco, Queretero, and Michocan. Perhaps more widely distributed as well.

## PROBLEMATICAL FORMS

### "BLAIR'S KINGSNAKE"
*Lampropeltis alterna "blairi"*
Flury, 1950

Thought to be nothing more than a color form of *L. alterna*, it is recognized by a smaller number of dorsal saddles (nine to 17) that are quite broad and rich orange-red in color, giving the snake a remarkably beautiful appearance.

Right: "BLAIR'S KINGSNAKE," *Lampropeltis alterna "blairi."* One of the most sought-after and undoubtedly most beautiful of the kingsnakes is this variety of the Gray-banded King. Diagnosed by having a small series of wide, orange-red saddles, it is known for a mild temper and easy breedability (although newborns often are difficult to get eating). Photo by R. G. Markel.

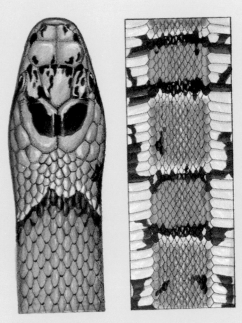

"BLAIR'S KINGSNAKE," *Lampropeltis alterna "blairi."* Artwork by John R. Quinn.

"BLAIR'S KINGSNAKE," *Lampropeltis alterna "blairi."* Reports of captive *"blairi"* have been nothing but complimentary. One keeper wrote that the animal was "...a very quiet snake that seldom resented handling." Zoo specimens have been raised on both white mice and lizards, which they would hunt down during night hours.

"BLAIR'S KINGSNAKE," *Lampropeltis alterna "blairi."* This animal varies not only within the Gray-banded Kingsnake species but even within itself! Depending on the locality of the specimen, the ground color may be a very light, ashy gray, or the dark, more slate-like gray seen here.

"BLAIR'S KINGSNAKE," *Lampropeltis alterna "blairi."* Described by Flury in 1950 (based on one dead specimen secured in southern Terrell County, Texas), Blair's King was originally considered a full species, *L. blairi,* but even at that time Flury had his doubts, commenting that he felt the snake might belong to one of a few other groups, including *doliata, alterna,* or possibly even *mexicana.*

PHOTO BY R. G. MARKEL.

"BOYLE'S BANDED KINGSNAKE,"
*Lampropeltis getula "boyli."* Apparently the
more popular of the two Cal King varieties,
"boyli" is nothing more than the name given
to the banded phase. For many years this
was thought to be a valid species, also
known in the vernacular simply as "Boyle's
Kingsnake."

PHOTO BY K. H. SWITAK.

"SOUTH FLORIDA KINGSNAKE,"
*Lampropeltis getula "brooksi."* Considered
by many to be a valid subspecies, this
attractive creature is the color phase of the
Florida King, *L. g. floridana*, found at the
southernmost edge of the range. Albinos of
this variety also exist.

PHOTO BY R. G. MARKEL.

"RINGED BAJA KINGSNAKE," *Lampropeltis
getula "conjuncta."* One of the more attractive
of the perplexing group of California
Kingsnakes, *L. g. californiae, conjuncta* is
fairly popular with hobbyists. For many years
it was thought to be a valid taxon, but since
has been judged a very melanistic race of
the standard ringed Cal King.

## "BOYLE'S BANDED KINGSNAKE"
*Lampropeltis getula "boyli"*
(Baird and Girard, 1853)

Known for many years as a full
species, "boyli" is now a dusty and
almost completely forgotten name
for the ringed form of *L. g.
californiae*. These days, both
hobbyists and scientists alike
simply refer to this animal as the
ringed or banded variety of the
California Kingsnake.

## "SOUTH FLORIDA KINGSNAKE"
*Lampropeltis getula "brooksi"*
Barbour, 1919

This name is applied to
specimens of *L. g. floridana* that
come from the extreme southern
part of the range. The dark parts
of the pattern are very, very
vague, and in some instances
completely absent, resulting in a
very golden, and consequently
very beautiful, animal.

## "RINGED BAJA KINGSNAKE"
*Lampropeltis getula "conjuncta"*
(Cope, 1861)

The Baja California Kingsnake
has for decades been considered
nothing more than a Baja variant
of Boyle's Banded Kingsnake,
*Lampropeltis getula "boyli,"* which
in itself is considered the banded
phase of the California Kingsnake,
*Lampropeltis getula californiae*
(confusing, huh?). Like *"boyli,"* it
is indeed banded, but with the
"lighter" markings being more
narrow and spaced further apart,
and rather than being a light to
medium yellow color they are
more of a medium to dark gray,
giving the snake a strongly
melanistic appearance (for which

both this snake and its close relative *L. g. "nitida"* are known).

### "BLOTCHED KINGSNAKE"
*Lampropeltis getula "goini"*
Neill and Allen, 1949

Also known as the Chipola River Kingsnake, this animal can be diagnosed by a relatively light background color and a count of 15 to 17 wide saddles these being brown but with a light yellow spot on each scale. The belly color is the same as that of the saddles, and with alternating dark patches. The head is fairly light, but the labials may have reduced dots or lines. Young often are heavily tinged with orange, some selectively bred specimens being more orange than anything else although the orange scales still have at least some dark coloration near the scale base. This snake is native only to the Chipola and Apalachiola River valleys in Florida and is considered by many to be an intergrade of *L. g. getula* and *L. g. floridana*.

### "STRIPED BAJA KINGSNAKE"
*Lampropeltis getula "nitida"*
Van Denburgh, 1895

Basically, this is the name applied to the striped or melanistic varieties of *L. g. californiae* that occur in Baja. In some very small ways both this snake and its sister the Banded Baja Kingsnake, *L. g. "conjuncta,"* have differences from *californiae*, but those differences simply are not strong enough to compel scientists to recognize both snakes as separate subspecies.

"BLOTCHED KINGSNAKE," *Lampropeltis getula "goini."* Commonly bred in the hobby, select examples of this snake often have heavy orange tinting, as seen on this newborn specimen.

"STRIPED BAJA KINGSNAKE," *Lampropeltis getula "nitida."* The general opinion of taxonomists concerning the Baja forms of the Cal King is that they are not genuine subspecies but simply darker forms of the more conventional subspecies. The ringed variant is known as the *"conjuncta"* form and the striped variant is the *"nitida"* form. In many *"nitida"* specimens, like the one shown, the vertebral stripe is almost totally obscured.

"OUTER BANKS KINGSNAKE," *Lampropeltis getula "sticticeps."* There are more than a few professionals who feel this snake is a valid subspecies. Admittedly, due to the fact that it is native to the Outer Banks islands of North Carolina, chances are this is true.

PHOTO BY R. G. MARKEL.

"DURANGO MOUNTAIN KINGSNAKE," *Lampropeltis mexicana "greeri."* So named because of its apparently only reliable locality—the mountains of Durango, Mexico—the name was given basically so hobbyists could recognize and relate to it.

PHOTO BY K. T. NEMURAS.

"NUEVO LEON KINGSNAKE," *Lampropeltis mexicana "thayeri."* This animal is also known as the "Variable Kingsnake" due to its immense amount of color and pattern variation. Specimens supposedly can be found on the eastern slope of the Mexican Plateau in the Miquihauna area of Tamaulipas.

PHOTO BY K. T. NEMURAS.

## "OUTER BANKS KINGSNAKE"
### *Lampropeltis getula "sticticeps"*
Barbour and Engels, 1942

Already considered by many to be a valid subspecies, this attractive little puzzler can only be found on Ocracoke and very likely the other islands of North Carolina's Outer Banks. It is believed to be a relict intergrade population of *L. g. getula* and *L. g. floridana*, and its appearance in some ways would suggest this. While it looks very much like *getula*, it does have a hint of *floridana* with its many light-centered scales, white spotting along the ventrolateral region, short middorsal crossbands, and head shape. The belly is also very dark. Adults reach a length of about 50 in/127 cm. Choice specimens of this animal, which are now being produced in captivity, are quite beautiful.

## "DURANGO MOUNTAIN KINGSNAKE"
### *Lampropeltis mexicana "greeri"*
Webb, 1961

Very similar in many ways to *L. mexicana*, *"greeri"* not officially considered a valid subspecies by most. Average adult length around 36 in/91 cm. It has a light buff ground color and about 33 black-edged red bands that are narrowly bordered with white. These bands are uninterrupted at their widest point, on top. There also is a distinct triangular or Y-shaped blotch on the neck. The ventral surface boasts a few very dark blotches. Ventrals average 202, and subcaudals around 60. It is a resident of the mountains of

PHOTO BY R. G. MARKEL.

"NUEVO LEON KINGSNAKE,"
*Lampropeltis mexicana "thayeri."*
Banding on this kingsnake can be very
thin or very broad, with a brick red to
orange coloration. On the broader
saddles, very light centers may occur, as
on the specimen shown here.

Durango, Mexico, hence the common name.

### "NUEVO LEON KINGSNAKE"
***Lampropeltis mexicana "thayeri"***
Loveridge, 1924

Also known as the Variable Kingsnake, the name is rather well-applied since the animal can vary greatly even within the same litter. The "standard" appearance, at least as far as hobbyists are concerned, involves a medium to light gray ground color with a series of thin orange red saddles, outlined first in black and then, just slightly, in white. Again, keep in mind that there are other forms as well, many greatly resembling the tricolored Milk Snakes, *L. triangulum*, while others have a strong melanistic tendency. Adults reach a length of about 36 in/91 cm.

"NUEVO LEON KINGSNAKE," *Lampropeltis mexicana "thayeri."* Passable to the layman as either a Desert Black Kingsnake, *L. g. nigrita*, or a Black Milk Snake, *Lampropeltis triangulum gaigae* (or, for that matter, a number of other, less-closely related snakes), this *"thayeri"* is wholly melanistic, a trait not uncommon in this animal.

PHOTO BY R. G. MARKEL.

# CONSIDERATIONS BEFORE PURCHASE

Regulations by city, county, and state will vary and should be checked out before acquiring your first specimen(s). Most local pet stores know the regulations and can assist you. Certain snakes may be legal in one state but not another, so it is best to check on the legality of owning snakes in your area. One source is your state's Fish and Wildlife Department, and there are others as well.

Are you purchasing snakes with future propagation in mind? Keep in mind that a single male can be bred to several females and therefore females command a higher price. Single females are not always easy to come by, especially

PHOTO BY W. P. MARA.

FLORIDA KINGSNAKE, *Lampropeltis getula floridana* (albino). A snake's head is a good place to look for early signs of ill health. Check around the eyes (mites, abrasions), mouth (cheesy secretions, swollen gums), and nostrils (nasal discharge, crustiness).

as adults. Generally females are easier to acquire after the hatching season (when their owners are more willing to give them up), but it is not uncommon to be given no other choice but to buy adults in pairs only. When purchasing newborns, depending on where you buy, you may have to leave a deposit before hatching has even started.

Raising juveniles can be a rewarding experience, seeing them grow to mature adults and then reproduce themselves, but it can be frustrating at times if they are poor feeders. Generally snakes that are captive-bred and are already established feeders will demand a higher price, but they may be worth it in the long run. Breeding loans are not uncommon in the higher-priced snakes, the "payoff" for each party being worked out when the neonates appear and the sex ratio is determined. All in all, ask yourself, what is the reason behind your purchase or acquisition? Is this going to be a pet, a display specimen, or a future breeding prospect?

Physical appearance of your prospective animal is indicative of its health. A basic physical examination is simple and can avoid costly veterinary bills in the future. Make a judgment on not only the condition of the animal you are considering, but the condition of all the other animals where your potential purchase is coming from. The animal(s) should be alert, fairly strong, and not overweight or overtly thin. Any snake that appears weak is to be avoided. Stay away from any animal that is wheezing or gasping for air. Bubbles or nasal discharge is an indication of infection. Gently examine the mouth. It should have a clean, white-pinkish appearance. Cheesy excretions, swellings, and bubbly mucus are indications of a serious (and potentially expensive) infection. How do the scales look? They should be clean, shiny, and have no bumps, wounds, sores, blisters, or scars. Look for mites on and under the scales and around the eyes, mouth, and nostrils. If you can, try to get a guarantee of the snake's health in writing. Most reputable dealers will do this, with the guarantee lasting around ten days. Before bringing home your purchase be sure you have an escape-proof cage complete with fresh water and a hiding place.

Snakes are expert escape artists, so whether your setup is a store-bought glass aquarium or a homemade enclosure, be sure it is secure. One method of housing that is inexpensive is the use of plastic shoeboxes or, for larger specimens, plastic sweaterboxes. These are lightweight, easy to clean, stackable when not in use, and by the time your collection reaches 50 or more animals you will appreciate the convenience of being able to work with them so easily. Drilling holes through the sides will provide adequate ventilation. There are several manufacturers of these boxes, so they are readily available in some pet shops.

If on the other hand you are displaying specimens you may want to go into a more elaborate setup. While this will be more visually esthetic, it will also be more expensive and more difficult to maintain.

PHOTO BY ISABELLE FRANCAIS, COURTESY OF TIM M. SCOTT.

After you purchase your kingsnake, be sure to house it separately because kingsnakes have strongly cannibalistic tendencies. You don't want to come home to an enclosure that previously held three kingsnakes only to find one very large one!

Two keys to keep in mind for the kingsnakes are that they need plenty of room and *they must be housed separately*. Substrates such as dried pine shavings, aspen, corn cob-type rodent bedding, and newspaper are all

FLORIDA KINGSNAKE, *Lampropeltis getula floridana*. Once you get a kingsnake feeding regularly it will become quite voracious and demanding. It is imperative that you have a steady supply of food items ready.

hungry snake that you can't feed, not to mention you are endangering the animal's welfare. Frozen and thawed mice as opposed to live ones may be an alternative if you can get your snakes to accept them. A successful method for weaning them onto these is to offer a live mouse first, then, immediately thereafter, one that has been thawed. Let the snake kill the live mouse first, then, as it searches for the head, remove the mouse and replace it with a frozen and thawed one. This whole weaning process may take time, but it will be worth it in the long run. Frozen mice can be purchased in quantity from any number of places. Your local pet shop should carry frozen rats and mice, and you should buy in bulk.

Now that you have a setup for your specimen(s) and a steady source of food, you need to take a look at the temperature requirements. A range of 80 to 85°F/26 to 30°C will suffice. Thermoregulation (temperature control) is important, as it encourages a feeding response and aids in digestion. A fluctuation of ten degrees in either direction may cause regurgitation or simply cancel out a snake's urge to eat. Two popular methods for heating include room heaters (space heaters), if you want to keep the entire collection at a constant range, and heat tapes, which can be used under one section of a particular enclosure so the snake can have the choice of either a warm area or a cooler one.

good choices, but cedar-based beddings will poison snakes. Aquarium gravel may look nice, but it needs to be washed often and is quite heavy. There are advantages and disadvantages to all substrates, but your choice really depends on the individual and how many specimens you have. Cleaning takes precedence over looks in my book, but if you can afford the time to keep exotic displays going, then more power to you. Once your collection grows to a great size, the priority becomes whatever it takes to keep the specimens clean and well-fed.

The continuous availability of food items should be assured before acquiring any specimens. It can be very frustrating to have a

# MAINTENANCE AND HOUSING

There are many types of enclosures available to the enthusiast. Cost certainly is a factor as to which kind you will choose, as is the "direction" of your collection. If you are going to keep only a few specimens for pets or as display animals, then you may want to invest a little more in the individual setups. If, on the other hand, you have a large collection or future breeding colony, then you may want to consider simpler, more conservative arrangements. Individual displays might include something like lock-top aquariums with internal display items such as rocks and/or bark, with an attractive substrate. Lighting adds to the effect and sometimes supplies heat. If you are planning on expanding your collection, then

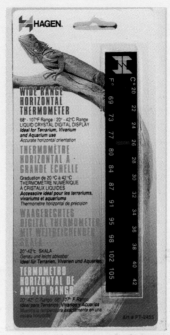

Keeping on eye on a kingsnake's ambient temperature is a must. To aid you in this particular area of snake husbandry, there are a few high-range thermometers that can be applied directly to the glass wall of an aquarium. Photo courtesy of Hagen.

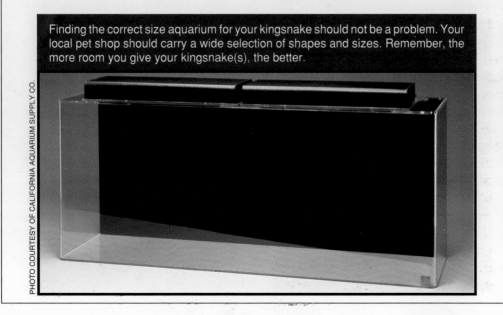

Finding the correct size aquarium for your kingsnake should not be a problem. Your local pet shop should carry a wide selection of shapes and sizes. Remember, the more room you give your kingsnake(s), the better.

PHOTO COURTESY OF CALIFORNIA AQUARIUM SUPPLY CO.

Re-usable cage liners are ideal for kingsnakes. They are offered in a range of sizes (to fit any size tank), are reasonably priced, and are easy to work with.

Natural substrates such as bark nuggets and bark mulch can be used with a number of kingsnake species. Such substrates are sold in your local pet shop and usually can be bought either in small bags or in bulk.

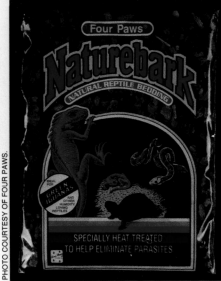

maybe a multiple cage unit will suit your needs.

A large collection requires more time and energy to maintain, so enclosures that are lighter in weight and more easily accessible should be taken into consideration. One such enclosure is the plastic shoebox, or, for larger specimens, the sweaterbox. One advantage to these is that there are no tight corners to clean. Such corners can also be hiding spots for tiny parasites. A second advantage is that they are lightweight, stackable, and inexpensive. Also, since space often is a problem for keepers, many specimens can be housed in a relatively small area.

Since kingsnakes cannot regulate their own body temperature, you must do it for them. 79 to 84°F/26 to 29°C is optimum for most kingsnakes, with a few subspecies able to live in slightly cooler temperatures. If you maintain a complete collection in one room, heating the entire room can serve the purpose. (Also, you can cool down the same room during hibernation.) For the heating of individual enclosures, there are several devices on the market, including under-tank heating pads, heated rocks, and spot lamps, but no matter what item you prefer, remember to leave an area where the specimen can avoid the heat if it wishes. Also, the effectiveness of any heating device will be enhanced if regulated by a thermostat.

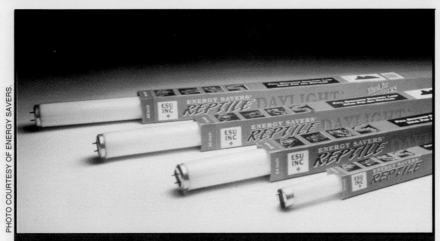

Providing a kingsnake with full-spectrum lighting is not *essential* to the animal's survival, but many keepers claim their animals live longer and have better breeding results when exposed to such light. Full-spectrum bulbs can be found at many pet shops.

Once cleaning becomes too laborious, it will take the fun out of maintaining a collection, transforming it into a burden rather than a pleasure. A large collection can become quite demanding, and small collections have a tendency to

Heating only a particular section of your kingsnake's enclosure by way of an undertank heating device is a sensible way of providing warmth. By leaving another section cool, you give the snake a choice.

expand. Design a simple, step-by-step cleaning method for yourself, with emphasis on minimal effort for maximum effect.

From the time you get your first snake, you should begin keeping records. Three-by-five cards with information such as when and where you acquired your specimen are important to have. Other valuable data include feedings, sheddings, the snake's size, weight, and sex, and its species and, when applicable, subspecies. Breeding information is also essential— date of copulation, date of egglaying, clutch sizes, date of hatchings or live births, percentage of eggs hatched, and so on. Also record illnesses and medications used. If you wish to get really fancy, there are cards available that are preprinted for this specific use.

# FEEDING

Kingsnakes usually are very easy to feed. While it is true many kingsnakes are ophiophagus (meaning they feed on other snakes, including other kingsnakes), they also have a strong preference for small mammals as well. In truth, kingsnakes as a whole have quite a varied diet. They will consume warm-blooded prey such as rodents and birds, plus cold-blooded items such as lizards, frogs, and, as mentioned, snakes. For this reason, kingsnakes must be housed individually. They are immune to native venomous snakes and will consume them as well, but this is not to say you should try obtaining venomous species as snake food! Even though the intervals between a kingsnake's feedings may vary in the wild, it is important to feed captive specimens on a steady basis. Acquiring a snake can be a rewarding experience, but maintaining it afterwards may become disheartening if you do not have a steadily available source of food, preferably mice, and preferably frozen and thawed.

There are some tricks to getting snakes to take thawed rodents. One is to offer a freshly killed rodent, and then, immediately thereafter, one that has been thawed. Another method is to dangle a freshly killed rodent in front of a snake and let the snake "kill" it. Hold on to the mouse's tail with forceps until the snake has a good grasp. When the snake lets go to search for the head, switch the freshly killed rodent with one that has been thawed. This works surprisingly well, and soon the snake(s) will be used to taking thawed-out mice all the time.

The two best ways to thaw out a frozen mouse are to either immerse it in a bowl of hot water (as hot as your tap can provide) for about 30 minutes (drying it off afterwards before offering), or simply let it sit out in the open (room temperature) overnight. Remember, a swallowed mouse that is still frozen on the inside will do a snake great harm.

PHOTO BY ISABELLE FRANCAIS, COURTESY OF PATRICIA C. LOLL.

"BLAIR'S KINGSNAKE," *Lampropeltis alterna "blairi."* Many keepers prefer to offer their kingsnakes pre-killed food items for reasons of safety—a live mouse could easily turn on a kingsnake that is not hungry and wound the serpent before the keeper has a chance to intervene.

The size of the meal offered is directly related to the size of the snake. Over-feeding or under-feeding will not be in your snake's best interests. Normally, a weekly feeding of one good-sized meal should suffice, with the number of mice offered being determined by the size of the individual. As a snake grows, increase the size of the meals. A snake continually consuming meals of the same size will not put on the weight and length that it would if the meal size were increased accordingly.

If one of your snakes does not feed well, several factors must be considered. The environment that you provide plays a large role in feeding responses. If the cage is warm, dry, and clean, most kingsnakes do fine in captivity, but if a specimen refuses to eat, the list of possible reasons is quite large— the snake could be in the middle of a shed; it may be injured or suffering some other form of ill health (parasites, etc.); a female might be gravid; the enclosure's temperature could be too low or too high; the snake may be insecure due to a lack of suitable hiding places; and perhaps the food item offered is simply wrong. Also, remember that a newly acquired specimen may not feed immediately but instead will need time to adjust to its new surroundings.

Methods of initiating a feeding response are better known as "tricks of the trade." One is to raise the temperature five to ten degrees. Ambient warmth is very important with kingsnakes. If the temperature varies too much, the

"BLAIR'S KINGSNAKE," *Lampropeltis alterna "blairi."* Pinkies are the ideal meal for young kingsnakes (although many will not accept them). Pinkies fulfill a kingsnake's dietary requirements and can be purchased in quantity.

feeding response not only may be altered, but even worse, a snake may regurgitate what it has already eaten.

Another trick is to ask yourself, when was the last time my snake shed? Most snakes do not feed during the shed cycle, but once it is over a snake will be quite hungry and spend much of its time searching for food. This is a perfect time to get a feeding response.

Females usually will refuse food during egg development, but once the eggs have been deposited, the

A word of warning to those who are ambitious enough to breed their own mice—a lot of space will be required, plus a lot of time and effort and a high tolerance to unpleasant odors. On the other hand, a high level of convenience will be afforded.

Lizards make great kingsnake food in spite of the fact that most keepers either don't want to offer them or simply can't afford to. However, the occasional pet-store anole, like the one shown, can be obtained at a reasonable price and should be included as a nutritious "treat" every now and then.

CALIFORNIA KINGSNAKE, *Lampropeltis getula californiae*. The dangers of leaving a kingsnake with other snakes—this Cal King has made a meal out of this Gopher Snake, *Pituophis catenifer*. While other snakes undoubtedly are highly nutritious for kingsnakes, it is impractical to regard them as a staple food item for many reasons.

For larger kingsnakes, rats make a good meal. Beware, however, that rats can be expensive, and furthermore a kingsnake may grow so fond of them that it will altogether abandon its liking for the more easily obtainable mice.

mother will have a voracious appetite. Remember that females will lose a great amount of body weight after egglaying, so you need to increase their food intake when they start feeding again.

Leaving a dead mouse at the opening of a hidebox at night has proven successful. "Scenting" is another effective approach—take a dead mouse and scent it with a dead lizard (frozen lizards may be used repeatedly), or simply place a pinkie in a container with some lizards for a short period. Try a mouse that hasn't been scented before going to scented mice, otherwise the snake may become dependent on the scented smell and then you'll have to scent the mice all the time.

If all else fails and it looks like the snake might die from starvation, the emergency alternative is force-feeding. The procedure is quite tricky. You have to hold the snake behind the head with forefinger and thumb while supporting the rest of the body so the snake does not dangle. Gently pry the mouth open with a smooth instrument or a free finger (this is when a second pair of hands comes in handy). Insert the mouse, head-first, into the mouth of the snake (use a mouse smaller than one the snake would normally consume if feeding on its own). The snake should grasp the mouse in its jaws and hang on. If it does, gently place it back into its cage. Hopefully the snake will finish the process and swallow the prey. If this does not happen, the force-feeding process will have to be repeated. Undoubtedly this will

PHOTO BY JEFF WINES.

CALIFORNIA KINGSNAKE, *Lampropeltis getula californiae* (albino). Be careful that you, the keeper, are not the focus of a hungry kingsnake. Many specimens tend to lose their normally mild tempers when feeding time comes around. If this should occur and the animal does not release its grip, do not try to tear it off; that could cause damage to the animal's teeth and gums. Instead, spray a little cold water in its face. If that doesn't work, a very tiny dab of rubbing alcohol on the snout will do the trick.

inflict some stress on the snake, but that's just how it goes. If the snake consumes the prey without too much fuss, place another food item in the enclosure next to it. It just might take a second course on its own.

If this "passive" force-feeding technique fails, you will have to resort to firmer measures. Lubricate a mouse, using either water or raw egg, and, after placing it in the snake's mouth, gently force the mouse down the throat with a blunt instrument and then massage the food item all the way down to the stomach. Replace the snake gently into the enclosure and do not bother it for the remainder of the day. Two other methods of force-feeding—the use of pinkie pumps and liquid feeding via a similar tube pump—may be used with small specimens.

If you are planning on maintaining a large collection, you may want to consider culturing your own mouse colony. First let's discuss the drawbacks—space requirements, odor, initial expense, and maintenance. The amount of space required for one "breeding group" (one male and three or four females) can be provided with a 10-gallon aquarium. Water usually is provided via a small bottle hung inside the cage. Points to remember include the fact that your mice will, quite frankly, stink, and any nearby places may be affected. This means, for example, if you keep them in your cellar and there's a vent leading from the mouse room to somewhere else in the house, an offensive odor will result, so always keep the mouse room well-ventilated. Also keep in mind that your mice need to be kept warm because cold mice very likely will not produce young.

# BREEDING

Snakes that are both in good health and have a proper captive environment will breed for you. Some snakes, regardless of their good health and careful husbandry, refuse to reproduce in captivity, but kingsnakes are fairly easy to propagate. Age, size, and weight of your specimens, plus hibernation, correct introduction of pairs, actual copulation, and gestation are all factors of successful reproduction.

The first step is sex determination. The most reliable way for an ordinary keeper to determine the sex of adult kingsnakes is by the use of a sexing probe. These are commercially available, made from stainless steel, and come in a variety of sizes for different-sized snakes. It is highly recommended that probing be done only by someone who has experience, the inexperienced party or parties learning from the experienced person.

The sexing of hatchlings, however, is a different situation. The use of probes is not recommended with newly hatched snakes because many of them are too small even for the smallest probes and thus probing them will not only injure them, it may kill them. The alternate method here is called "popping." This is done by applying gentle pressure to the base of the tail and pushing upward. This should expose the hemipenes in males. Females are identified by two tiny dots at each end of the vent. Popping is only perfected by experience, and even the best of us are not always 100% accurate.

It goes without saying that sexually mature animals are essential for successful breeding. An absolute minimum age of two years is required for a kingsnake;

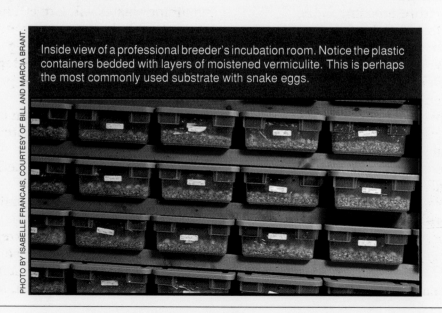

Inside view of a professional breeder's incubation room. Notice the plastic containers bedded with layers of moistened vermiculite. This is perhaps the most commonly used substrate with snake eggs.

PHOTO BY ISABELLE FRANCAIS, COURTESY OF BILL AND MARCIA BRANT.